WORKBOOK

—— FOR ——

Grace for Purpose Prayers

Deepen your dialogue with the God of the impossible

June Willison

This Book Belongs To

Disclaimer

Introduction

This workbook is designed to act as a practical guide to the original book. The aim of this workbook is to help anyone implement, practicalize, and deepen their faith in the God of the impossible.

This workbook is divided into five parts. Each part contains a daily suggested Bible reading plan for

Spiritual growth,
Personal breakthrough,
Family and friends,
And for the nation at large.

This workbook is designed to help you deepen your relationship with God and grow in your faith. It is also a valuable resource for anyone who is looking forward to growing in their prayer life and for anyone who is looking for prayers for specific needs or situations.

Suggested 7 Day Bible Reading Plan On Prayers for Spiritual Growth

Day 1: Psalm 51:10

Day 2: Psalm 86:11

Day 3: Proverbs 3:5-6

Day 4:   2 Peter 3:18

Day 5:   John 15:5

Day 6:   2 Timothy 1:7

Day 7: 2 Corinthians 3:18

Spiritual Growth

In life, we all want to grow financially, mentally, and physically, but we forget the most important aspect of life, which is growing spiritually with God and in his knowledge. Spiritual growth with God is a journey of deepening your relationship with divine knowledge. It is a process of learning, reflection, and transformation that leads to a greater understanding of yourself and your purpose in life.

The first step to growing spiritually with God is to establish a personal relationship with Him. This can be done through prayer, attending worship services, and engaging in other spiritual practices. By opening your heart and mind to God, you create a space for Him to work in your life.

As you deepen your relationship with God, you will begin to experience a greater sense of peace, joy, and fulfillment. You will also gain a deeper understanding of your true nature and purpose in life. This understanding can lead to a sense of clarity and direction, as well as a greater sense of meaning and purpose.

By taking time to examine your thoughts, feelings, and actions, you can identify areas where you need to grow and change. You can also gain insights into your strengths and weaknesses and develop a deeper sense of self-awareness.

Date:

Todays Scripture

Lessons

Lord am greatful for...	Prayer Request

Which aspects of your spiritual existence do you consider require the most growth?

_____

_____

_____

_____

What does spiritual growth mean to you?

_____

_____

_____

_____

_____

Persornal Notes

Date:

Todays Scripture

Lessons

Lord am greatful for...	Prayer Request

How do you manage to keep your prayer practice consistent?

What challenges have you encountered on your spiritual growth path, and how have you conquered them?

Persornal Notes

EXERCISE

Spend some time in peaceful reflection, concentrating on breathing and cleansing your thoughts of any distractions. Meditation can assist you in connecting with your inner self and developing a more profound sense of calm and stillness.

Date:

Todays Scripture

Lessons

Lord am greatful for...	Prayer Request

In addition to prayer, which spiritual practices do you take part in?

_____

_____

_____

_____

How has your bond with God changed as you've grown spiritually?

_____

_____

_____

_____

Persornal Notes

Date:

Todays Scripture

Lessons

Lord am greatful for...	Prayer Request

How do you approach spiritual development in every aspect of your life?

How do you incorporate your spiritual development into your interactions with others?

Persornal Notes

EXERCISE

Record your feelings and ideas regarding your spiritual path. This can assist you in learning more about yourself and your connection with the spiritual.

Date:

Todays Scripture

Lessons

Lord am greatful for...	Prayer Request

How do you strike a balance between spiritual development and other aspects of your daily existence, such as your job or family?

_____

_____

_____

_____

HWhat part do communities play in your spiritual development?

_____

_____

_____

_____

Persornal Notes

Date:

Todays Scripture

Lessons

Lord am greatful for...	Prayer Request

How has your perspective on prayer changed over time?

How has prayer helped you get through tough times?

Persornal Notes

EXERCISE

Develop a sense of thankfulness by concentrating on all the positive aspects of your life. Start a thankfulness notebook or simply take some time each day to think about things you're grateful for.

Date:

Todays Scripture

Lessons

Lord am greatful for...	Prayer Request

How are you able to recognize when you're growing spiritually?

How has your spiritual development influenced other aspects of your life?

Persornal Notes

Persornal Breakthrough

In our lives, prayers for personal breakthrough with God are a way for individuals to connect with God deeply and seek His guidance.

This can go a long way toward helping them overcome any obstacles and challenges they may encounter in their lives. These prayers can be powerful tools for spiritual growth and transformation and can lead to a deeper relationship with God.

One of the most important aspects of prayer for personal breakthrough is faith. Believing that God has the power to intervene and help us in our struggles is essential for effective prayer. It is important to approach prayer with humility and an open heart, recognizing that we are in need of God's help and guidance.

When praying for personal breakthrough, it can be helpful to focus on specific areas where we need help and guidance. This may include areas such as relationships, finances, career, health, or spiritual growth. By identifying the specific areas where we need breakthrough, we can bring them before God and ask for His help and guidance.

Suggested 7 Day Bible Reading Plan On Prayers for Personal Breakthrough

Day 1: Matthew 7:7

Day 2: Mark 11:24

Day 3: Philippians 4:6

Day 4:   John 15:7

Day 5:   Psalm 17:6

Day 6:   Matthew 21:22

Day 7: James 5:16

Date:

Todays Scripture

Lessons

Lord am greatful for...	Prayer Request

What does personal breakthrough refer to you, along with what do you expect to accomplish utilizing prayer?

_____

_____

_____

_____

What are the particular areas of yourself in which you are eager to see progress?

_____

_____

_____

_____

Persornal Notes

Date:

Todays Scripture

Lessons

Lord am greatful for...	Prayer Request

How has prayer assisted you in the past in overcoming hurdles, and in what ways can you apply those teachings to today's circumstances?

What is your greatest fear when it comes to praying for personal breakthrough, and how might prayer help you conquer that fear?

Persornal Notes

EXERCISE

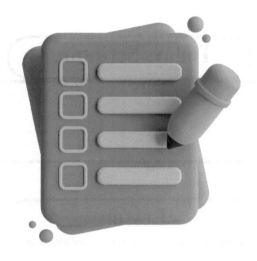

Take some time to think about those parts of your life in which you have become stuck or need to make a breakthrough. Make a list of them and be as descriptive as possible.

Date:

Todays Scripture

Lessons

Lord am greatful for...	Prayer Request

What is the significance of faith in the prayers of life, and in what ways can you grow your faith to reach personal breakthrough?

What measures can you take in order to make prayer a more frequent and ongoing part of your life?

Persornal Notes

Date:

Todays Scripture

Lessons

Lord am greatful for...	Prayer Request

Write about an occasion when you had a breakthrough that you knew was due to prayer.

_____

_____

_____

_____

_____

What are some of the most frequent misunderstandings regarding prayer, and how may you dispel them in your own life?

_____

_____

_____

_____

_____

Persornal Notes

EXERCISE

Write a confessional prayer in which you beg God to pardon you for any sins or wrongdoings that are impeding your progress.

Date:

Todays Scripture

Lessons

Lord am greatful for...	Prayer Request

What Bible scriptures or passages motivate you when you pray for personal success? and why?

_____

_____

_____

_____

_____

How can you engage others in your prayer journey, and in what way may their support assist you in reaching personal breakthrough?

_____

_____

_____

_____

Persornal Notes

Date:

Todays Scripture

Lessons

Lord am greatful for...	Prayer Request

Write an abdication prayer in which you let go of your own ambitions and allow God to guide you to the triumph He has prepared for you.

_____

_____

_____

_____

_____

Write about an occasion when you were about to give up and how prayer encouraged you to endure.

_____

_____

_____

_____

Persornal Notes

EXERCISE

Write a forgiveness prayer, asking God for guidance as you forgive anybody who hurt or offended you in the past.

Date:

Todays Scripture

Lessons

Lord am greatful for...	Prayer Request

What routines or habits can you develop to make prayer a more meaningful and significant part of your life?

_____

_____

_____

_____

_____

What specific techniques can you use to improve spiritually with the goal of preparing for your own breakthrough?

_____

_____

_____

_____

_____

Persornal Notes

Family and Friends

We should learn to show love to our friends and family because they are the most important part of our lives before anything else, and one way to show this love is by praying for them.

Praying for your loved ones is an amazing way to show them how much you genuinely care about them. It is a method of connecting with God in order to obtain blessings, wisdom, and safety for those you cherish. Prayer is a global language that crosses religious, cultural, and geographic borders, and it may provide comfort and calm to both those praying and those being prayed for.

You are able to convey appreciation for the people who are in your life, appreciate their successes and failures, and ask for goodness and guardianship for their health when you pray for your family and friends.

You can pray for their well-being, security, happiness, prosperity, and spiritual progress and have faith that your prayers will be granted in the most favorable manner for them.

Praying for friends and relatives can also help you build stronger bonds with them. It may be a method to express your encouragement and empathy, as well as to let them realize you are supporting them even if you are separated by distance.

It may also be a method to strengthen your own faith and confidence in God, as well as to feel connected and purposeful in your life.

Suggested 7 Day Bible Reading Plan On Prayers for Personal Breakthrough

Day 1: Numbers 6:24-26

Day 2: Ephesians 3:16

Day 3: Romans 15:13

Day 4: Psalm 28:7

Day 5: Psalm 20:4

Day 6: Proverbs 3:5-6

Day 7: Psalm 16:8

Date:

Todays Scripture

Lessons

Lord am greatful for...	Prayer Request

Recall a moment when your prayers for a relative or friend were answered. What took place, and exactly how did it affect your prayer life?

_____

_____

_____

_____

Create a prayer, particularly for a loved one, relative, or friend who is experiencing or going through a difficult moment. What words of encouragement or consolation would you offer?

_____

_____

_____

_____

Persornal Notes

Date:

Todays Scripture

Lessons

Lord am greatful for...	Prayer Request

Examine the significance of appreciation in your close relationships and prayers. How can praying with appreciation improve your relationships?

Share a prayer routine or activity that you use to support and encourage your family and friends. How does this exercise strengthen your bond with them?

Persornal Notes

EXERCISE

Write a diary of prayers for your family and loved ones. Make a list of particular prayers for each person and keep it up-to-date.

Date:

Todays Scripture

Lessons

Lord am greatful for...	Prayer Request

Recall a moment when you were at your breaking point for words to pray for a family relative or acquaintance. How did you surmount this obstacle and find comfort in prayer?

Choose a family member or acquaintance who has influenced your spiritual path positively. Write a Thanksgiving prayer for their presence in your life.

Persornal Notes

Date:

Todays Scripture

Lessons

Lord am greatful for...	Prayer Request

In your requests for family and friends, consider the theme of surrender. Whenever it's related to their wellness, how can you let go and believe in a greater power?

_____

_____

_____

_____

_____

Share a time when you had an intimate relationship with a family member or friend while praying. What made the moment so meaningful to you?

_____

_____

_____

_____

_____

Persornal Notes

EXERCISE

Write down 10 things you appreciate about your family and friends. Say a thankful prayer for every single thing on the list.

Date:

Todays Scripture

Lessons

Lord am greatful for...	Prayer Request

Describe a moment when the prayers you offered for a family relative or acquaintance weren't answered as you hoped. How has this event influenced your view of prayer and faith.

Examine the effectiveness of praying intercessory prayers for your loved ones. How does praying for them affect your spiritual growth?

Persornal Notes

Date:

Todays Scripture

Lessons

Lord am greatful for...	Prayer Request

Share a prayer routine that you use to foster tranquility and cooperation between your loved ones. How does this practice improve your relationship with them?

Say a prayer offering safety for your loved ones, asking for heavenly protection and direction in their lives. What unique good fortune would you like to bestow upon them?

Persornal Notes

_____

_____

_____

_____

_____

_____

_____

_____

_____

_____

EXERCISE

Write individual intercession cards for each of your closest friends and family members. Make a prayer for their health and special needs. Keep these cards accessible as an indication to pray for them on a regular basis

Date:

Todays Scripture

Lessons

Lord am greatful for...	Prayer Request

Recall a moment when you experienced tremendous peace of mind when praying for a friend or relative. How did this event strengthen your faith in prayer?

Recall a time when you observed prayer's transformational effect in the life of a friend or relative. What inspired and strengthened your personal prayer practice as a result of this?

Persornal Notes

Nation

It is essential for us to pray for the nation's abundance, health, and security. Prayers for the nation become much more meaningful at times of tragedy or instability. It is a source of peace and comfort, allowing people to discover strength and perseverance in the face of adversity.

It provides a place for people to come together and find solace in their shared conviction that a higher force can lead and defend their country.

Praying for the nation frequently addresses issues like harmony, equity, growth, and knowledge for leaders. Praying for the welfare of citizens, the safety of vulnerable groups, and the healing of conflicts.

These prayers express the collective desire to construct an open-minded, fair, and understanding society in which all individuals can prosper while contributing to the greater good.

Regardless of one's religious views, praying for the nation is an important habit because it allows individuals to refocus on their responsibilities as moral citizens and to develop an awareness of civic responsibility.

By coming together to offer prayer, people are able to direct their goals and goodwill towards the enhancement of their nation and its residents.

Suggested 7 Day Bible Reading Plan On Prayers for the Nation

Day 1: 2 Chronicles 7:14

Day 2: Psalm 33:12

Day 3: Proverbs 14:34

Day 4: Psalm 67:1-2

Day 5: Psalm 72:8

Day 6: Psalm 85:6

Day 7: 1 Timothy 2:1-2

Date:

Todays Scripture

Lessons

Lord am greatful for...	Prayer Request

What particular issues does your country confront that necessitate God's intervention and guidance?

_____

_____

_____

_____

_____

In what manner have you prayed for the international leaders' knowledge and discernment?

_____

_____

_____

_____

_____

Persornal Notes

Date:

Todays Scripture

Lessons

Lord am greatful for...	Prayer Request

How can you advocate for your country equity and righteousness?

_____

_____

_____

_____

What prayers can you give for those in uniform and first responders' security and well-being?

_____

_____

_____

_____

Persornal Notes

EXERCISE

Take a couple of steps to reflect on your country's present status. Create a prayer in which you express your anxieties and aspirations for its wellness and advancement.

Date:

Todays Scripture

Lessons

Lord am greatful for...	Prayer Request

What specific sectors of your country require prayer for stability, development, and good fortune?

_____

_____

_____

_____

How can people pray for the educational system of the country to be changed and prepared to fulfill the requirements for forthcoming generations?

_____

_____

_____

_____

Personal Notes

Date:

Todays Scripture

Lessons

Lord am greatful for...	Prayer Request

What are your prayers for the abolition of hardship, homelessness, and inequality in the country?

How do you pray for an end to criminal behavior, violence, and the safeguarding of society's weakest members?

Persornal Notes

EXERCISE

Make a list of particular concerns or obstacles that your country is experiencing. Spend time in prayer, interceding for each of these issues separately

Date:

Todays Scripture

Lessons

Lord am greatful for...	Prayer Request

What particular prayers do you give for the recovery and restoration of catastrophe-affected people and communities?

How do you pray for an environment of empathy, kindness, and togetherness to pervade your nation?

Persornal Notes

Date:

Todays Scripture

Lessons

Lord am greatful for...   Prayer Request

What particular prayer can you give for the recovery and restoration of damaged relationships and households in your country?

_____

_____

_____

_____

How would you advise people to pray for an increase in opportunities for meaningful work and fair remuneration for all citizens of the country?

_____

_____

_____

_____

Persornal Notes

EXERCISE

Begin a gratitude notebook for prayers for your country. Put down a minimum of three aspects of your nation that you are thankful for each day and say prayers of thanksgiving.

Date:

Todays Scripture

Lessons

Lord am greatful for...	Prayer Request

What prayers would you advise someone to say for the safety and well-being of children, the elderly, and the weak in society?

_____

_____

_____

_____

How can people pray for a rebirth of faith, spiritual rejuvenation, and moral restoration in the country?

_____

_____

_____

_____

Persornal Notes

Made in United States
Troutdale, OR
10/09/2023

13544034R00066